Scholastic BookFiles

SO-ACU-796

The Watsons Go to Birmingham—1963

by Christopher Paul Curtis

Amy Griffin

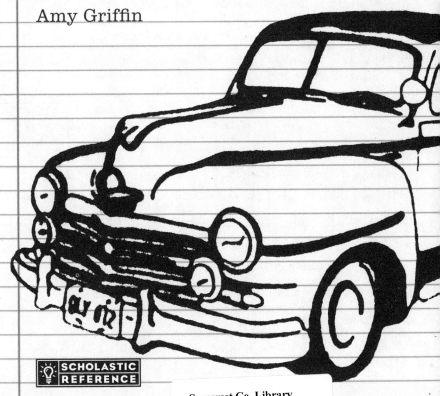

Library of Congress Cataloging-in-Publication Data

Scholastic BookFiles: A reading guide to
The Watsons Go to Birmingham—1963
by Christopher Paul Curtis/Amy Griffin.   p. cm.

Summary: Discusses the writing, characters, plot, and themes of this 1996 Newbery Honor Book. Includes discussion questions and activities. Includes bibliographical references (p.).

1. Curtis, Christopher Paul. The Watsons Go to Birmingham—1963—Juvenile literature.   2. African-American families in literature—Juvenile literature.   3. Civil rights movement in literature—Juvenile literature.   4. Birmingham (Ala.)—In literature—Juvenile literature.   5. Racism in literature—Juvenile literature.   [1. Curtis, Christopher Paul. The Watsons Go to Birmingham—1963   2. American literature—History and criticism.]   I. Title.   II. Series.

PS3553.U6943W34   2004

813′.6—dc21   2003042842

0-439-29802-4

10 9 8 7 6 5 4 3 2 1   04 05 06 07 08

Composition by Brad Walrod/High Text Graphics, Inc.
Cover and interior design by Red Herring Design

Printed in the U.S.A.   23
First printing, March 2004

Contents

"The Watsons will always be special to me because it broke me out of the warehouse I was working in. I'm doing something that I want to do, finally."

–Christopher Paul Curtis

When Christopher Paul Curtis received a Newbery Honor for his first book, *The Watsons Go to Birmingham—1963*, he achieved something that many authors spend their whole lives working toward. How does an author accomplish so much with his first book? Hard work? Determination? Talent? In Curtis's case, it was a combination of all three.

Christopher Paul Curtis was born on May 10, 1953, in Flint, Michigan. He is the second of five children born to Herman E. Curtis, a doctor, and Leslie Curtis, a homemaker. Both of his parents loved to read, and so did Christopher, but he had trouble finding books about African-American kids like himself.

In school, one of Curtis's favorite teachers was Ms. Suzanne Henry-Jakeway, his third-grade teacher. He has said that his favorite class was history and his favorite book was *To Kill a Mockingbird* by Harper Lee.

When Dr. Curtis's patients weren't able to pay him enough to support his family, he went to work at Fisher Body Flint Plant No. 1, where he worked on an assembly line, putting together cars. After Christopher graduated from high school in 1971, he began working with his father at the Fisher Body plant. It was supposed to be only a summer job to make some money before he started college in the fall, but the money was too good to pass up. Curtis worked full-time on the assembly line for thirteen years, hanging eighty-pound doors on Buick cars. At night, he attended classes part-time at the Flint campus of the University of Michigan, working toward a degree in political science. While he was a student there, Curtis received the Avery Hopwood and Jules Hopwood Prize for major essays for an early draft of *The Watsons Go to Birmingham—1963*. Curtis loved the idea of being a writer, but with a full-time job and school at night, how could he ever find time to write?

At Fisher Body, the guys on the line alternated hanging the car doors: One man would hang a door, then his partner would hang a door, and they would repeat the process again and again, hanging a total of sixty doors every hour and never getting a very long break. But Curtis and his partner came up with a plan: If one of them hung *every* door for a half hour straight, rather than alternating, the other man could rest or do whatever he liked for a half hour every hour. For Curtis, this meant a half hour of writing for every half hour of hanging doors! Once he and his partner started using this system, Curtis found that the regular writing schedule helped him become more confident in himself as a writer. He also found that the time he spent writing at work took him to another place in his mind, away from his tedious job.

He has said that he believes the hard work of an assembly line gave him the discipline to be an author.

After leaving the factory, Curtis held several jobs while he continued to take classes. He worked as a campaign worker, a maintenance man, a customer service representative, a warehouse clerk, and a purchasing clerk. In 1993, Curtis's wife, Kaysandra, told him that he "better hurry up and start doing something constructive with his life or else start looking for a new place to live." Kaysandra said that for one year she would support the family while he wrote his book.

With that challenge set before him, Curtis spent most of the next year at the public library, working on the manuscript that would become *The Watsons Go to Birmingham—1963*. At the end of the year, he took a chance and submitted the manuscript to a national contest for unpublished authors. An editor plucked Curtis's project out of the huge pile of manuscripts and chose it for publication. *The Watsons* went on to be named not only a Newbery Honor Book—one of the most respected awards for a children's book—but also a Coretta Scott King Honor Book, an American Library Association Best Book for Young Adults, and was the only book for young readers to make *The New York Times* list of top 100 books of the year. And how did Christopher Paul Curtis follow up the huge success of his first book? He wrote *Bud, Not Buddy*, which won the 2002 Newbery Medal—the highest honor a children's book author can receive! Curtis, who received his bachelor of science degree from the University of Michigan in 2000, continues to write and is currently at work on his third book, *Bucking the Sarge.*

How *The Watsons Go to Birmingham—1963* Came About

"I've always felt like inside I was a
writer. Whatever else I've done, I'm
Christopher Curtis/Writer. It's one of
those situations where if you follow
your dreams, sometimes you're
extremely lucky and things do come
true, and I feel extremely lucky with
what has happened."

—Christopher Paul Curtis

Flint, Michigan, is home to many people who are originally from the South. Christopher Paul Curtis had heard some of his friends at the factory talk about driving south when they visited their relatives. Rather than splitting up the trip and staying overnight someplace along the way, they'd drive for many hours straight—however long it took to get there.

Curtis always wondered if he would be able to do the same, so when his wife's sister moved to Florida, he decided to give it a try. His wife wanted to plan the trip every step of the way, but he was set on driving twenty-four hours straight! Soon, Christopher, his wife, Kaysandra, and their son Steven were on their way to

Florida. Little did they know that the trip would become the basis of Curtis's first book.

Curtis says, "That's how the story got started. It was about a family taking a trip and the year was 1963, but the story was called *The Watsons Go to Florida* at the time. Then I went back and worked on it, but once I got the family to Florida, nothing happened. So I set it aside for a while, until my son brought home a poem by Dudley Randall called "Ballad of Birmingham," about the bombing of the Sixteenth Street Baptist Church. As soon as I heard it, I said, 'Ah! The Watsons want to go to *Birmingham!*' and I wrote the rest of the story." While the story is not autobiographical, Curtis has said that he can see parts of himself in both Kenny and Byron Watson.

Each day, Curtis worked on the manuscript in the children's section of the local library. At night, his son Steven would help out by typing what he'd written by hand earlier in the day.

But Curtis didn't have a literary agent, so he wasn't sure how to go about getting the book published. He knew that he would have to find some way for someone at a publishing house to read his story. To accomplish that, Curtis submitted the book to Delacorte Press's Contest for a First Young Adult Novel. His editor, Wendy Lamb, recalls opening piles of submissions to the contest and seeing the title *The Watsons Go to Birmingham—1963*, "words that filled [her] with curiosity and dread; words that instantly evoked the church bombing where young girls died in Sunday school. Well, [she thought] this person was ambitious, trying to write about something terrible, something important." She decided to take a second look later, and while the characters in the book made it too young to qualify for the contest, she loved it so much that Delacorte decided to publish it anyway.

Everyone—teachers, librarians, critics, and children—loved the book, too, and it went on to be one of the most successful books published in 1995.

An Interview with Christopher Paul Curtis

"I hope I'm writing the kind of books that I would have liked to read as a child."

—Christopher Paul Curtis

◆ *When you were in school, were you known to be a good writer?*

Yes. I didn't necessarily like to write, though. And when I was in school, there wasn't a lot of emphasis put on creative writing. We would mostly write essays and term papers. My problem was getting motivated to do it. Once I got it done, I was pretty good at it.

◆ *What was your favorite class?*

Probably history, but I think it always depended on the teacher. A particular teacher can make something very interesting.

◆ *You have said that* To Kill a Mockingbird *was your favorite book as a child. Do you still read books that are intended for young readers?*

Yes, I read a lot of books for kids now that I've found out I'm an author for kids. I want to know what everybody else is doing.

◆ *Are there any recent books for young readers that have impressed you?*

Yes. *Hush* by Jacqueline Woodson.

◆ *I have read that one of your favorite authors is Toni Morrison. Can you explain what you like most about her writing?*

It's her use of language; the beauty of her words keeps you coming back.

◆ *What do you like most about writing for children?*

It takes me back to my childhood, which was a very happy time for me. It brings back a lot of memories. I find it very relaxing. When I work, I just sit there and smile.

◆ *Do you take time off between writing books?*

After I finished *The Watsons Go to Birmingham—1963*, I started *Bud, Not Buddy* right away. I was back to working in a warehouse, and I didn't want to do that. I figured I would have to publish ten books before I could quit my job so I thought, "Let me get right on this." With the book I'm working on now, *Bucking the Sarge*, I have taken time off.

♦ *When will* Bucking the Sarge *be published?*

It will come out in fall 2004.

♦ *What do you like to do when you're not writing?*

It depends on where I am in the book. Toward the end of a book I'm pretty focused on it, but at other times, I love to play basketball. I love listening to music and traveling.

♦ *Do you ever get blocked? For example, do you ever have trouble thinking of what might come next in the book you're currently writing, or what your next book will be about?*

I never do, and if I did I would never admit it to myself. I think once you tell yourself you're blocked, then you've got problems. And I think being blocked means that there's a flaw in something you've written, and it just doesn't flow naturally. What you have to do is give yourself some time, move away from it for a while, and your mind will work on it when you're not even thinking about it. The solution will come to you. You go back into the story, find out where it went wrong, and go at it from there. If I'm having trouble with one story, I always have another project going, so I can jump over to that. And that way I don't stop writing. The most important thing is not to stop. You just have to keep going and you'll work things out.

♦ *You originally had planned to have the Watsons drive to Florida instead of Alabama, but changed your mind after your son came*

*home with Dudley Randall's poem "Ballad of Birmingham," about
the bombing of the Sixteenth Street Baptist Church. Were there any
other surprises that came up as you wrote the manuscript?*

The way I write everything is a surprise. I don't outline. I don't
know where the story is going to go. Everything that goes on is
kind of a revelation to me, which is one of the fun parts. I know
I've really got the story when the narrator comes to me as soon as
I sit down and he tells me what's going to happen next.

◆ *What was the most difficult part of the book to write?*

Starting a book is always the hardest. Being the kind of author
who doesn't outline, if I start to write a book, I don't know where
those words will end up in the story—the beginning, middle, or
end. I just know I have to get it down and get the story flowing.

◆ *With which character do you have the most in common?*

I think that both Byron and Kenny have certain traits that are
from me. I'm the older brother in my family, and my younger
brother would swear that Byron is an accurate picture of me.

◆ *What are you working on now?*

I'm in the early stages of a new project—it's not exactly a sequel
to *Bud, Not Buddy*, but it's got some of the same characters. I'm
trying to do a story from a girl's point of view.

Chapter Charter: Questions to Guide Your Reading

The following questions will help you think about the important parts of each chapter.

Chapter 1

- What interesting language does the author use to describe how cold it is in Flint?
- How does Hambone Henderson try to discourage Wilona from marrying Mr. Watson? What do you think Mr. Watson thinks of Hambone? How can you tell?
- What kind of relationship does Kenny have with his brother, Byron?

Chapter 2

- Why do you think Kenny is afraid when he realizes that the reading he has been chosen to do will be for Byron's class?
- What happens after the reading that surprises Kenny?
- Why does Kenny see Rufus, the new boy on the bus, as his "personal saver"?

Chapter 3

- Why is Kenny hesitant to spend time with Rufus?
- How was Rufus's life in Arkansas different than it is in Flint?
- Why do you think Kenny is friends with LJ, even though LJ isn't nice to him?

- Why does Kenny end up thinking that Rufus is a better friend than LJ?

Chapter 4
- What kind of relationship does Kenny have with Joetta? Can you give examples of things that happen between them that make you think that?
- Why do you think Byron stops Larry Dunn from giving Kenny a "Super Maytag" when Byron often plays similar tricks on Kenny himself?
- How does the author make the reader sympathize with Larry Dunn?
- Have you ever had a problem with a bully at your school? How did you work it out?

Chapter 5
- Why do you think Mrs. Watson speaks "Southern-style" when she gets angry?
- If you were Mrs. Watson, how would you punish Byron when he plays with fire?
- Do you agree with Mrs. Watson's way of punishing him? Why?

Chapter 6
- Why do you think Byron gets sick after he kills the mourning dove?
- Why does he get angry at Kenny so suddenly?
- How does the author show that Byron is not as tough as he pretends to be?

Chapter 7

- What is your first clue about Byron's latest misdeed?
- Why do you think Byron keeps doing things that his parents have forbidden?
- When Byron misbehaves, who do you think handles the situation better, Mr. or Mrs. Watson? Why?
- In addition to thinking it is ugly, why does Mrs. Watson object to Byron's new hairdo?

Chapter 8

- Why do you think Kenny is so eager to have a real mustache like his dad's?
- Why do the Watsons think sending Byron to Alabama will help him to behave better? Do you think it will work?

Chapter 9

- Besides not wanting to get hooked on country music, why do you think Daddy decides to install the TT-700 in the Brown Bomber?
- Why do you think Joetta wants to keep the angel from Mrs. Davidson in a drawer?
- Why do you think Mrs. Watson is so careful with her planning of the trip, such as where the family is going to stay?

Chapter 10

- Why does Kenny ask for a second serving of Kool-Aid, even though it tastes bad to him?
- Why do you think Kenny feels scared when they're driving through the mountains?

Chapter 11

- How is Birmingham like Flint? How is it different?
- Have you ever traveled to meet relatives who lived far away from you? How did it feel when you first met them?
- How does Byron behave when he meets Grandma Sands? Were you surprised by his behavior?

Chapter 12

- How does Mrs. Watson act differently when she is with her mother in Alabama compared with how she acts at home in Flint?

Chapter 13

- How does Byron change when the Watsons arrive in Alabama?
- Why do you think he changes so suddenly?
- Why does Kenny decide that it is okay to go into the water at Collier's Landing?
- What did you learn about Byron's feelings for Kenny in this chapter?

Chapter 14

- How does the author describe the scene at the church, after it has been bombed?
- Why do you think Kenny sees the Wool Pooh in the church after it has been bombed?
- Why does Joetta think that Kenny has changed his clothes?

Chapter 15

- Why does Byron spend so much time with Kenny when they come back to Flint?
- Why does Kenny start going to the World-Famous Watson Pet Hospital so often?
- How does Byron help Kenny to feel better at the end of the book?

> "All of my family sat real close
> together on the couch under a
> blanket.... Momma was the only one
> who wasn't born in Flint so the cold was
> coldest to her. All you could see were
> her eyes too, and they were shooting
> bad looks at Dad."
>
> —*The Watsons Go to Birmingham—1963*

The Watsons Go to Birmingham—1963 follows the Watson family's experiences in Flint, Michigan, and their 1963 trip to Birmingham, Alabama.

Kenny Watson, the narrator, is ten years old, the same age Christopher Paul Curtis was in 1963. The book begins on a cold, winter day, with the whole family huddled together on the couch under a blanket. Because their heater isn't working they decide to spend the night at their aunt Cydney's. When Kenny and his brother, Byron, are sent outside to scrape the ice from the car windows, Byron does very little scraping, preferring to instead admire himself in the side mirror of the car. He makes the mistake of kissing his reflection, and his lips instantly freeze to the mirror! It's up to Kenny to save his brother. He calls for his parents, and eventually they are able to detach Byron's lips from the mirror.

Kenny is often the subject of bullying at school because he has a lazy eye. Larry Dunn is the biggest bully in the school, but sometimes Kenny is even bullied by Byron and his friend Buphead. One day on the bus, Kenny thinks that his "personal saver" has arrived in the form of a new kid named Rufus. Rufus has a thick Southern accent and shares his clothes with his little brother; Kenny believes that surely Rufus will become the new target of the other kids' teasing. Kenny is right that Rufus's arrival takes some of the bullies' attention away from him. But when he finds himself becoming good friends with Rufus, suddenly it doesn't feel like much of a relief after all.

Meanwhile, Byron's behavior gets worse and worse: He skips school, and does things against his parents' wishes. Byron and Buphead are too "cool" for school and often play hooky. "Give my regards to Clark, Poindexter," he says, letting Kenny know that he won't be at school that day. Once, when Momma discovers that Byron has been playing with matches, after being told again and again not to, she is at her wit's end. She is so angry that she tells Byron that she's going to burn him as punishment. Joetta and Kenny try to protect Byron from Momma, but she just says, "Don't you see how Momma has to help Byron understand how dangerous and painful fire can be? Don't you see we've tried everything and nothing seems to get through that rock head of his?"

Kenny thinks that Byron will get into more trouble than ever when he comes home one day with a hairstyle known as a conk, which Momma and Dad have told him not to get. Momma asks Byron, "Did those chemicals give you better-looking hair than me and your daddy and God gave you?" Dad shaves Byron's head, and Momma calls her mother in Birmingham, Alabama. They have decided that Byron will spend the summer with Grandma Sands, who is known to be very strict. Kenny says, "The biggest reason Byron and Joey and me thought they'd never send him to Alabama was because we had heard so many horrible stories about how strict Grandma Sands was. The thought of living with her was so terrible that your brain would throw it out as soon as it came in." Byron is horrified by the idea of going to Alabama, but there's no way for him to avoid it.

Momma carefully plans the car trip from Flint to Birmingham. Dad installs an Ultra-Glide machine to play records in the Brown Bomber, the family's nickname for their car. The trip is to take three days, and Momma is careful to pack plenty of food and water so that they won't have to stop in an area where they might come across people who are hostile or even violent. The family is aware of the problems in the South—the racial division and tension between black people and white people—but Momma and Dad are still convinced that sending Byron there is the right decision. Kenny tells the reader, "We'd seen the pictures of a bunch of really mad white people with twisted-up faces screaming and giving dirty finger signs to some little Negro kids who were trying to go to school. I'd seen the pictures but I didn't really know how these white people could hate some kids so much." Dad says, "Kenneth, I know you're going to miss Byron, we all will, but son, there are some things that Byron has to learn and he's not learning them in Flint, and the things he is learning are things we don't want him to."

In the end, the trip takes far less than three days: Dad drives straight through, while the rest of the family sleeps. Almost immediately after the Watsons arrive at Grandma Sands's house in Birmingham, Byron's behavior improves. Kenny takes this opportunity to indulge in some of his own misbehavior. Against Grandma Sands's warnings, he goes swimming at Collier's Landing and comes close to drowning in a whirlpool. Luckily, Byron saves him just in time. Kenny is convinced that Byron had to fight an imaginary monster called the Wool Pooh.

A few days later, Kenny stays home while Joetta heads off to Sunday school at the local church. After hearing a loud noise, he goes outside and sees that people are running toward the church. There's been an explosion, and many people have been injured. In a daze, Kenny enters the church to search for Joetta. In the basement, he sees a patent-leather shoe like his sister's sticking out of some rubble. He struggles to pull the shoe out of the rubble, all the while imagining that he's fighting the Wool Pooh for it. Then he returns home, thinking that Joetta has been killed. When she appears at his bedroom door, he thinks that she is a ghost.

The Watsons (including Byron) return to Flint very soon, but everyone—especially Kenny—is haunted by the church bombing. Kenny spends most of his time alone behind the couch. Byron tries to help Kenny. He tells him, "Kenny, things ain't ever going to be fair. How's it fair that two grown men could hate Negroes so much that they'd kill some kids just to stop them from going to school? How's it fair that even though the cops down there might know who did it nothing will probably ever happen to those men? It ain't. But you just gotta understand that that's the way it is and keep on steppin'."

Thinking about the plot

- How does Kenny's life change in the book?
- Describe Byron's transformation in Birmingham.
- Why do you think Christopher Paul Curtis chose to include the bombing of the Sixteenth Street Baptist Church, something that *really* happened, in a book that is mostly fictional?

"[Momma] always blamed [Dad] for bringing her all the way from Alabama to Michigan, a state she called a giant icebox."

—*The Watsons Go to Birmingham—1963*

The Watsons Go to Birmingham—1963 takes place in Flint, Michigan; Birmingham, Alabama; and along Interstate I-75, which is the route the Watsons take on their trip to Alabama. Flint is a midsize industrial city, home to many factories and car assembly plants like Fisher Body Flint Plant No. 1, where Christopher Paul Curtis and his father worked. Birmingham is also a city with a large number of steel factories. In 1963, Birmingham was a focal point for the civil rights movement.

Most of the action takes place in the Watson home in Flint, in the Brown Bomber on the way to Birmingham, and at Grandma Sands's house in Birmingham. Although Flint is a city, Kenny's house has a yard where Kenny and his friend LJ Jones can dig holes to bury his toy dinosaurs. And their neighborhood is friendly enough that the family is allowed to keep a running tab for their groceries at Mr. Mitchell's, paying for everything at the end of the week when Mr. Watson gets his paycheck.

Flint, Michigan, has a much colder climate than Birmingham, Alabama, where Momma was born. She often complains about the cold to Dad. When the family arrives in Birmingham, Kenny remarks that it is "like an oven." But in 1963, the differences between Flint and Birmingham were far more serious than just the weather. Throughout the country, African Americans were often subjected to discrimination, but nowhere was it as extreme as in the South. There, many public areas, such as restaurants, schools, playgrounds, motels, bathrooms, and drinking fountains, were racially segregated, meaning they were to be used either by blacks or by whites, but not by both. The facilities for blacks were always of poorer quality. Many communities and states passed laws that affected African Americans' opportunities for schooling, housing, and employment. Interracial marriages were prohibited, and laws and tests were created to prevent African Americans from voting.

Until the Civil War was fought in the 1860s, most African Americans in the United States were slaves. After slavery was outlawed, it took a very long time for African Americans to begin to get the same rights and opportunities as white people. One of the first steps was the passage of the Thirteenth, Fourteenth, and Fifteenth constitutional amendments in the late 1860s and 1870. These amendments promised citizenship rights for African Americans by abolishing slavery, redefining U.S. citizenship to include African Americans, and prohibiting federal or state governments from interfering with a citizen's right to vote based on his or her race. Later, the Civil Rights Act of 1875 stated that there should be equal accommodations for blacks and whites in public facilities, except schools. Unfortunately, not everyone followed these new laws, especially people in the South. So for many years, these legislations did little to improve the day-to-day life of blacks in America.

An important step toward ending racial discrimination was the 1954 case *Brown* v. *Board of Education of Topeka, Kansas.* In this court case, the U.S. Supreme Court ruled that public schools could no longer be segregated. However, white racists fought the ruling, threatening black students who attended schools that had been formerly all white. The most extreme confrontation took place at Central High School in Little Rock, Arkansas, in 1957; President Dwight D. Eisenhower ordered the Arkansas National Guard to protect the black students. The national media coverage of the daily developments at Central High brought much-needed attention to Little Rock and to the civil rights situation in general.

At the time of *The Watsons Go to Birmingham—1963,* the civil rights movement, which had begun in the late 1950s, was gaining momentum. Those involved in the civil rights movement used various types of protest in an attempt to gain equal treatment for blacks. And it was working: Not since the Reconstruction period after the Civil War had such important breakthroughs in equal-rights legislation been achieved.

Led by black leaders including Dr. Martin Luther King, Jr., Thurgood Marshall, John Lewis, Medgar Evers, and Fannie Lou Hamer, groups of black and white activists took a stand, riding together on interstate buses and sitting together at whites-only lunch counters. Using nonviolent protest methods like marches, sit-ins, and boycotts, these leaders furthered their cause. The success of the civil rights movement infuriated white racists, who in turn resorted to violent behavior, even murder, trying to scare people away from their goal of reaching racial equality. The civil rights movement was at its height in 1963. On August 28 of that year, 200,000 people marched on Washington, D.C., to pressure Congress to pass the Civil Rights Bill, and heard Martin Luther King, Jr., deliver his famous "I Have a Dream" speech.

The next year, President Lyndon B. Johnson signed the Civil Rights Act of 1965 (also called the Voting Rights Act of 1965). Voter registration and requirements had always been considered a matter of local and state control. The new law changed that, allowing the federal government to get involved if necessary. The law worked. Most Southern states voluntarily opened their registration lists to blacks; in others, the Justice Department took control. Soon after, African Americans, who comprised a majority in parts of the South, were electing black mayors and sheriffs and supervisors. With the Civil Rights Act and 1968's Fair Housing Act, which granted citizens the right to live wherever they wanted and could afford, the civil rights movement helped many African Americans obtain better jobs and housing.

One of the most shocking crimes committed during the civil rights movement was the bombing of the Sixteenth Street Baptist Church in Birmingham, Alabama, on September 15, 1963. When a bomb went off during Sunday school, four young girls—Addie Mae Collins, Denise McNair, Carole Robertson, and Cynthia Wesley—were killed. Curtis depicts this bombing in *The Watsons Go to Birmingham—1963* and dedicates the book to those girls. Curtis says, "When I was around ten years old and the civil rights movement was just beginning, my father was very active in it and he did a lot of traveling with the UAW [United Auto Workers]. For some reason that has been very vivid in my mind, so that's probably the thing that I remember most about my childhood."

To the Watsons, Flint feels like a safe haven from the violence of the South. But despite the situation in Birmingham, Momma is still convinced that it is right for Byron to be sent there. "You're going to like Birmingham, Byron. It's a lot different than Flint. . . . Your grandma tells me it's quiet in our old neighborhood, she says that that stuff on TV isn't happening around her. It's just like I remember it being, it's safe, it's quiet."

Dad doesn't seem to believe that Birmingham is as safe as Momma does, however. He's honest with Kenny, Byron, and Joetta about the fact that African Americans are treated badly in the South, and that they are often subjected to violence. Momma explains the plan for their trip to Birmingham and that they'll have to be selective about where they stop. Kenny asks why. Dad responds, in an imitation of a hillbilly accent, "'Cuz, boy, this he-uh is the deep South you-all is gonna be drivin' thoo. Y'all colored folks cain't be jes' pullin' up tuh any ol' way-uh and be 'spectin' tuh get no room uh no food, yuh heah, boy? . . . Whas a mattah wit' choo, you thank this he-uh is Uhmurica?" Dad knows that the family might come across some people in the South who won't treat them fairly and that they might be denied service at restaurants or motels along the way.

Curtis uses dialects to establish the differences in the settings of Flint and Birmingham. A dialect includes the characters' vocabulary, grammar, and pronunciation, and is unique to where they live. When Momma is particularly scared, frustrated, or angry, she uses what Kenny refers to as "Southern-style" language. Even though she has lived in the North, in Flint, for many years, when she is very emotional, she can't help but speak in the way she did when she lived in Birmingham.

Dad imitates a Southern dialect when he makes fun of Hambone Henderson, one of Momma's suitors when she was younger and lived in Alabama. Henderson tried to persuade Momma not to move to Flint with Dad, telling her that there weren't any other African Americans there, and that it would be too cold for her since she was used to living in Alabama's warmer climate: "Don't believe I seen nan one colored person in the whole dang city. You a 'Bama gal, don't believe you'd be too happy living in no igloo."

But in the end, when they arrive in Birmingham, Kenny realizes that maybe Birmingham and Flint aren't so different after all. "Birmingham looked a lot like Flint! There were real houses, not little log cabins, all over the place! And great big beautiful trees. Most of all, though, there was the sun."

Curtis has used Flint as the setting for both of his published books; his third and fourth books, which he is in the process of writing, are set there as well. Curtis says, "Flint is a fascinating city, in many ways it's emblematic of many of the so-called Rust Belt American towns; it has had tremendous booms and terrifying busts. It is rich in history and fertile ground for a writer. When I'm asked why all of my stories have taken place in Flint, I answer, 'Why not?' There are so many untold stories there. And that is true of every city and town."

Thinking about the setting

- How are Birmingham and Flint different? How are they similar?

- How does a change in setting change the characters' relationships to one another?

- Why might Momma have wanted to leave the South, despite the fact that she'd spent her whole life there?

[Momma said,] "You know Birmingham is a good place, and I don't mean just the weather either. The life is slower, the people are friendlier—" "Oh yeah," Dad interrupted, "they're a laugh a minute down there. Let's see, where was that 'Coloreds Only' bathroom downtown?"

—*The Watsons Go to Birmingham–1963*

Themes are the main ideas behind a book or other literary work. *The Watsons Go to Birmingham—1963* has several themes of varying importance, including racism, prejudice, and discrimination; family relationships; growing up; friendship; humor; and grief.

Racism, prejudice, and discrimination

Very early in *The Watsons Go to Birmingham—1963*, it is clear to the reader that racism and prejudice are major themes of the book. Certainly the quotation that opens this chapter is a tip-off that, even in 1963—about one hundred years after the Civil War and the end of slavery—the South was still a place where African Americans experienced a great deal of discrimination.

In the middle of the night during their trip to Birmingham, the family pulls over at a rest stop in Tennessee. It's very dark because they are in the mountains, far away from any city, but the Watsons are more scared of the people they might come across in this part of the country than they are of the dark. Kenny and Byron decide to go to the bathroom in the woods. Byron tells Kenny, "Man, they got crackers and rednecks up here that ain't never seen no Negroes before. If they caught [you] out here like this they'd hang you now, then eat you later." When he says that the people would eat Kenny, Byron is exaggerating, of course, but at this time in the 1960s, the threat of violence against African Americans was very real.

The Watsons arrive in Birmingham right before the Sixteenth Street Baptist Church bombing, one of many bombings of churches attended by African Americans that took place in the South during this period. Kenny goes to the church to try to find Joetta, who went there for Sunday school. He says, "I looked into the church and saw smoke and dust flying around like a tornado was in there. . . . I could see Bibles and coloring books thrown all over the place. . . . I could see a shiny, shiny black shoe lying halfway underneath some concrete." Kenny thinks that the shoe is Joetta's because she'd worn shiny black shoes to church that morning. When Kenny leaves to walk back home, he says, "I walked past people lying around in little balls on the grass crying and twitching, I walked past people squeezing each other and shaking, I walked past people hugging trees and telephone poles, looking like they were afraid they might fly off the earth if they let go. I walked past a million people with their mouths wide-opened and no sounds coming out." By placing his fictional family in the midst of something that really happened, Curtis helps the reader to understand what it was like for the people who were actually there.

Family relationships

The Watsons are an unusually close family, with strong emotional connections. The relationship between Byron and Kenny goes through a surprising change in the novel. At the beginning, Byron seems to dislike Kenny and often tries to use his position as older brother to get out of doing things that are his responsibility. When the boys are supposed to share the job of scraping ice off the Brown Bomber's windows, Kenny says, "I'm not going to do your part, Byron, you'd better do it and I'm not playing either." Byron's response is, "Shut up, punk." Clearly Byron feels superior to his little brother, and is planning to get out of his responsibility knowing that Kenny will eventually give in, as he has in the past. But this time, Byron ends up in a difficult position; Byron's lips become stuck to the Brown Bomber's side mirror and the only one who can help him is Kenny. Rather than using this situation to his advantage, Kenny quickly comes to his brother's aid. "I could have done a lot of stuff to him. If it had been me with my lips stuck on something like this he'd have tortured me for a couple of days before he got help. Not me, though," Kenny says, "I nearly broke my neck trying to get into the house to rescue Byron."

Throughout the book, there are many instances in which the reader glimpses Byron's true feelings about Kenny. It is only at the end of the story, when Byron helps Kenny through his grief about the Birmingham church bombing, that we see real evidence of just how much he loves his little brother. When Kenny truly needs Byron's support, Byron is there for him.

Byron and Momma also share an important relationship. One of the most intense scenes in the book is after Momma discovers that Byron has been caught playing with fire after being told again and again not to. For his punishment, she plans to burn his fingers.

> We all nearly jumped through the roof when the snake-woman voice came back into the room and said, "Joetta, move away from him." Momma was carrying a piece of paper towel, a jar of Vaseline and a Band-Aid in one hand and a fresh, dry book of matches in the other. She wasn't even going to take him to the hospital! She was going to set him on fire, then patch him up right at home!

This harsh punishment is the high point in their constant struggle for power.

Finally, Momma and Dad decide to make a huge financial sacrifice that they feel is necessary for the good of the family: They take Byron to Birmingham, where he immediately starts to behave better and obey his parents. Wilona Watson's relationship with her mother, Grandma Sands, is very close. "Grandma Sands and Momma would get yakking to each other and we could only understand half of the things that they said." These close family relationships help the Watson family overcome the difficult obstacles they face during the course of the book.

Growing up

From the very beginning of *The Watsons Go to Birmingham—1963*, it seems clear to the reader that Kenny is the "good boy" in the family and Byron is the "bad boy." Byron often threatens Kenny and joins forces with his best friend Buphead to bully Kenny. Kenny, of course, has little defense against his older brother. As the good one, he helps his mother and does well in school.

But as the story progresses, we see that perhaps Byron isn't such a bad boy and that Kenny isn't all good. When Kenny reads from a book in front of Byron's class, he is convinced that Byron will beat him up or hurt him in some way; instead, Byron is proud. And at the end of the story, Byron takes the role of comforting Kenny through his grief. For his part, Kenny also disobeys his parents when he decides to swim at Collier's Landing. In that scene, Byron protects Joetta by taking her to another part of the river to swim. "Here was a chance for another Fantastic Adventure and [Byron] was going in the wrong direction . . . He was acting real dull and square," Kenny says. "Maybe Byron was getting sick of having more Fantastic Adventures, but I figured I was getting old enough to have some myself." Ironically, once the Watsons arrive in Birmingham, it is Kenny who disobeys, rather than Byron. Kenny, the good boy, has decided that now that he's getting older, perhaps he wants to break the rules, just as Byron had earlier in the story.

Friendship

To Kenny's surprise, he and Rufus Fry become close friends. Rufus is a much better friend to Kenny than LJ Jones, who is always trying to trick Kenny. But one day on the bus Kenny makes a terrible mistake; everyone is laughing because Rufus and his little brother, Cody, share clothes. Kenny starts laughing, too, in front of Rufus. "Rufus shot a look at me. His face never changed but I knew right away I'd done something wrong. I tried to squeeze the rest of my laugh down." After a few days, Kenny goes to Rufus's house and asks him to play dinosaurs. But Rufus refuses and tells Kenny, "I thought you was my friend. I didn't think you was like all them other people." Only after Momma gets involved are the problems smoothed over and Rufus and Kenny get back to being friends. During the course of the book, Kenny learns what friendship really means, and how to be a better friend to Rufus. He comes to understand that what he had with LJ was not really friendship after all.

Humor

Humor plays a significant role in *The Watsons Go to Birmingham—1963*. Curtis uses humor to help the characters get through the many difficult situations in the book, be it the possibly dangerous trip to Birmingham or Byron's punishment for getting a conk hairstyle. But sometimes the humor is there purely for fun, like when Byron's lips get stuck after he kisses himself in the frozen car mirror, or in Byron's story about frozen Southerners, which he tells in order to convince Joey that she needs to wear many layers of winter clothes. "[T]here ain't nothin' more horrible than seein' hundreds of dead, froze-up Southern folks crammed up inside a garbage truck. . . . So Joey, don't be cryin' and whinin' when you put all them clothes on, it would break my heart to see my own family froze solid so's they got throwed in one them fake garbage trucks." Of course, Joey doesn't think this story is at all funny, and Kenny is not sure sure about it either, but the reader understands that Byron is just making it up to get Joey to cooperate.

Dad uses humor at the very beginning of the story when the family's heater is broken. He tells the kids about "Hambone" Henderson, Wilona Watson's old boyfriend. "Me and your granddaddy called him [Hambone] because the boy had a head shaped just like a hambone, had more knots and bumps on his head than a dinosaur. So as you guys sit there giving me these dirty looks because it's a little chilly outside ask yourselves if you'd rather be a little cool or go through life being known as the Hambonettes." The story makes everyone laugh and forget for a while just how cold their house is.

Grief

When the family returns home to Flint after the bombing at the Birmingham church, Kenny takes to sitting behind the couch in the Watsons' living room, a place that Byron calls the World-Famous Watson Pet Hospital. "He started calling it the World-Famous Watson Pet Hospital after we noticed that if something bad happened to one of our dogs or cats they just automatically knew they had to crawl in that space and wait to see if they were going to get better." Kenny spends his time there because he is expecting that the "magic powers" that often make his dogs and cats feel better will work on him, too. Kenny feels guilty because after he knew about the church bombing, he went home rather than trying to find Joetta. But Joetta hadn't even been inside the church when the bomb went off because she'd followed a stranger who she thought was Kenny away from the church. The time Kenny spends alone behind the couch allows him to grieve about the bombing and also to work through the guilt that he feels about his actions that day.

Momma and Dad deal with their own grief as well. "Some of the time they were mad, some of the time they were calm and some of the time they just sat on the couch and cried." But along with having to face their own feelings about the church bombing, Mr. and Mrs. Watson have to think about how to help their children grieve. They encourage Kenny to spend more time with Rufus and ask Byron and Buphead to take Kenny with them when they play basketball. What we learn is that grief is an emotion that everyone deals with differently; each of the Watson characters reacts in a specific way to their experience with the church bombing.

Thinking about the themes

- What do you think is the most important theme of *The Watsons Go to Birmingham—1963?* What are some of the other themes?
- When Kenny admits that he has treated Rufus badly, how does that help to correct the situation?
- What are some other important family relationships in *The Watsons Go to Birmingham—1963?*

T he *Watsons Go to Birmingham—1963* focuses primarily on the Watson family—Kenny, Byron, Joetta, Momma, and Dad—but also includes several other important characters.

Here is a list of the characters, followed by a brief description of each of the main characters.

Kenny Watson	ten-year-old boy, the story's narrator
Byron Watson	Kenny's thirteen-year-old brother
Joetta Watson	Kenny's younger sister
Wilona Watson/Momma	Kenny's mother
Daniel Watson/Dad	Kenny's father
Grandma Sands	Kenny's grandmother, Wilona's mother
Buphead	Byron's friend
Larry Dunn	Byron and Kenny's classmate
Rufus Fry	Kenny's friend
LJ Jones	Kenny's friend

Kenny Watson: Ten-year-old Kenny is the narrator of *The Watsons Go to Birmingham—1963*. This means that everything we read is described from Kenny's point of view. The middle child of the Watson family, Kenny is an excellent student and is trusted by his parents. He craves their approval and is thankful when his parents pay particular attention to him. "I loved when

Dad talked to me like I was grown-up. I didn't really understand half the junk he was saying, but it sure did feel good to be talked to like that!"

While many of the adults in the story take a particular liking to Kenny because he is well-behaved and also a good reader and student, his peers are not so kind. Kenny has a lazy eye—an eye that doesn't focus as well as the other—and they take this as a sign of weakness. Kenny is in the fourth grade and attends the same school as his brother and sister. He is often picked on by his classmates, which is even more frustrating because his older brother, Byron, one of the two oldest kids at Clark Elementary, is so respected by the other kids at the school. Kenny notes that having Byron for a brother "would make me a prince or a real strong angel or something but it didn't work that way, I was just another fourth-grade punk. I guess having the school's god as my brother did give me some kind of special rights but not a whole bunch."

But sometimes Byron surprises Kenny. At one point in the book, Kenny recalls a time in second grade when he was asked to do a reading from Langston Hughes in front of Byron's fifth-grade class. Kenny was mortified. He was so worried about Byron's reaction that he read very quickly through the passages to get it over with. But in the end, Byron wasn't mad at all; in fact, he was proud. "He punched me kind of soft in the arm and said, 'At least you oughta make 'em pay you for doin' that mess. If it was me they'd be comin' out they pockets with some foldin' money every time they took me around.'"

During the story, we learn that Kenny is not altogether loyal. His friendship with Rufus is the best indicator of this trait. While Kenny is perfectly willing to be friends with Rufus in secret, when the other kids on the bus are laughing at Rufus one day, Kenny joins in, hurting Rufus's feelings. "Rufus shot a look at me. His face never changed but I knew right away I'd done something wrong. I tried to squeeze the rest of my laugh down," Kenny says.

Another trait unique to Kenny's character is his fondness for exaggeration. We know this from the very first page of the book, when he says, "It was so cold that if you spit, the slob [spit] would be an ice cube before it hit the ground. It was about a zillion degrees below zero." Of course it's not actually a zillion degrees below zero, but by exaggerating, Kenny lets the reader know that it is *very* cold!

All of Kenny's individual qualities form a realistic character to whom readers can relate. Through him, Christopher Paul Curtis has created a character that is simultaneously funny, flawed, and ever-changing.

Byron Watson: At age thirteen, Byron Watson is constantly challenging his parents' wishes. Like any teenager, he tries to see how far he can go without receiving any punishment. The changes Byron goes through are very important to the plot of *The Watsons Go to Birmingham—1963*. It is because of his unmanageable behavior that Momma and Dad decide to go through with sending him to Grandma Sands. They feel that they have no other choice but to take him away from Flint and the bad influences he has found there. Despite his behavior, Kenny and Joetta still look up to their older brother. "Larry Dunn was king of the kindergarten to fourth grade only because Byron didn't care about them. Larry was the king of Clark . . . but Byron was a god," says Kenny.

Throughout the story, we see hints of Byron's true caring nature, like when he is proud of Kenny's reading, or when he makes the older kids play basketball with Kenny, or when he gets sick after killing the dove. "Maybe there were magic powers hiding in the way your older brother made all the worst thugs in the neighborhood play basketball with you even though you double-dribbled every time they threw you the ball," Kenny says. But what is most shocking to the Watson family is how quickly Byron's behavior changes once they reach Birmingham and Grandma Sands. "The way Byron kept his head down and was smiling and saying 'Yes, ma'am' this and 'No, ma'am' that, it looked like he had surrendered before the first punch was thrown." And by the end of the book, when he helps Kenny through his grief after the church bombing, Byron has become a kind of adviser to Kenny. In the last few pages, after Byron has talked Kenny into coming out from his hiding place behind the couch, he says:

It's 'bout time you cut this mess out, Momma and Dad beginning to think your little behind is seriously on the blink. Today is the day you check out of the World-Famous Watson Pet Hospital. Don't let me catch you back there no more. You ain't got no cause to be ashamed or scared of nothing. You smart enough to figure this one out yourself. Besides, you getting the word from the top wolf hisself; you gonna be all right baby bruh. I swear for God.

Wilona Watson/Momma: Momma is the source for both humor and tension in *The Watsons Go to Birmingham—1963*. She regularly reminds Dad that if it were up to her she'd still be living in her hometown of Birmingham. She is a caring mother, but a tough one; she often feels that the three children are getting out of her control, especially Byron. And she loses control herself sometimes, as in the scene where she threatens to burn Byron as punishment for playing with matches.

When Momma feels that she is being challenged, she quickly lets the kids know who's in charge; they can sense the change in her because she starts talking "Southern-style," something she also slips into when she is afraid, nervous, or angry.

Momma is just as much in charge of the family as Dad; she organizes every detail of the family trip to Birmingham because she is worried that they could possibly meet trouble along the way. "Momma had everything planned about the trip, everything! Where we'd eat, when we'd eat, who got baloney sandwiches on Day One . . . She'd figured out how long we could hold ourselves between going to the bathroom, how much money we'd spend on hamburgers, how much was for any emergencies, everything." Despite her controversial ideas about punishment, Momma is a good mother to the three kids and is the glue that holds the family together.

Daniel Watson/Dad: Dad is another source of humor in *The Watsons Go to Birmingham—1963*. He often tries to ease a tense situation by making his family laugh, for instance, when they are freezing cold in the first scene of the book, or when they are traveling to Birmingham and worrying about what they might encounter along the way. "I swear I've been looking in the rearview mirror and wondering where my babies were and where these three bad-dispositioned, sour-faced, middle-aged midgets came from," he says toward the end of the trip. Even when he must punish Byron for getting a conk hairstyle without permission, Dad's sense of humor never disappears. After he shaves off all of Byron's straightened hair, he comes down the steps. "Mrs. Watson," he said, "I'd like to introduce you to your long-lost son from Siam, His Royal Highness, Yul Watson!" (Dad is referring to Yul Brynner, who played the bald king in the movie *The King and I*.) But Dad wants Byron to know that the situation is serious and tells him, "This is it, By. You're old enough now and you've been told enough, this time something's going to be done."

Joetta Watson: Even though Joetta is the youngest of the Watson family, she shows great spirit, strength, and intelligence. She does not hesitate to stand her ground—even if it means standing up to Momma. When Byron gets in trouble for playing with matches, "Joey" is the first to protect him from Momma. "Joey spread her arms out to the side like a traffic cop and stood between Momma and Byron. 'No, Mommy, wait . . .'"

At another point in the novel, the Watsons' neighbor, Mrs. Davidson, gives Joey an angel figurine, telling her that she has named the angel after Joey. The angel is white and Joey is upset that Mrs. Davidson has named it after her. "Mrs. Davidson said it reminded her of me, but it didn't look like me at all." Rather than letting Mrs. Davidson know how upset this has made her, Joey politely accepts the angel, and later places it in her sock drawer, where she won't have to look at it.

Grandma Sands: Grandma Sands (Momma's mother) lives in Birmingham in the same house Momma grew up in. Grandma Sands is known to the Watson kids as a tough woman. When they finally meet her in Birmingham, they're a bit taken aback. "I was expecting a troll," Kenny says. "I thought Grandma Sands would be bigger than Dad, I thought she'd be foaming at the mouth like she had rabies." But instead, "What came out was a teeny-weeny, old, old, old woman that looked just like Momma would if someone shrank her down about five sizes and sucked all the juice out of her!" Grandma Sands has a very close relationship with her daughter Wilona; they not only share a mother-daughter relationship, but are also very good friends.

Rufus Fry: When Rufus and his little brother walk onto the school bus one morning, Kenny is sure that they will become the new targets for Clark Elementary's bullies, and will take some of the pressure off him. "As I looked at this new boy with the great big smile and the jacket with the holes in the sleeves and the raggedy tennis shoes and the tore-up blue jeans I knew who he was . . . I knew God had finally sent me some help, I knew God had finally sent me my personal saver." Rufus and his brother often share clothes, which lets us know that they are probably quite poor. He is protective of his little brother and very innocent compared to the other kids at Poindexter. While Rufus is hurt by Kenny's treatment of him, he does find it in himself to forgive Kenny and to trust him once again.

Thinking about the characters

- Which character changed the most during the course of the book? Why do you think that?

- How is your family similar to the Watsons? Different? How so?

- How does Christopher Paul Curtis let the reader know that Kenny is not all good and that Byron is not all bad?

It's a winner!

The Watsons Go to Birmingham—1963 was named a Newbery Honor Book in 1996. The Newbery Medal is one of the highest achievements in children's literature; Newbery honors are given to books that are also deemed worthy of special attention. Both are given annually by the American Library Association. The book was also named a Coretta Scott King Honor Book that same year. The Coretta Scott King Award is presented annually by the Coretta Scott King Task Force of the American Library Association's Social Responsibilities Round Table. It is given to authors and illustrators of African descent whose distinguished books promote an understanding and appreciation of the "American Dream."

Most people agree that Curtis is an excellent writer. One book reviewer from *The Horn Book* praised Curtis's ability to realistically describe Byron and Kenny's sibling relationship, as well as to weave together fictional characters and a real-life setting. The reviewer wrote, "Curtis's control of his material is superb as he unconventionally shifts tone and mood, as he depicts the changing relationship between the two brothers, and as he incorporates a fictional story." According to a starred review in *School Library Journal*, Curtis's "totally believable child's view of the world will make this book an instant hit."

However, judging literature is a very personal endeavor. People have different, individual tastes and like different things. While there has been very little negative criticism of *The Watsons Go to Birmingham—1963*, there has been some. For example, one reviewer noted that the time spent on the bombing scene and its aftereffects was too short: ". . . in two pages with a brief description the church is bombed. Then in two more days it's back to normal."

Thinking about what others think about
The Watsons Go to Birmingham—1963

- Do you think that *The Watsons Go to Birmingham—1963* seems like an award-winning book? What other Newbery Medal–winning or Newbery Honor books have you read? Did you like *The Watsons Go to Birmingham—1963*? Why or why not?

- Did you find the Watson family and their relationships with one another to be realistic?

- Do you agree that there should have been more time spent on the bombing and its aftereffects? Were there other parts of the book that you felt were either too short or too long?

Here are some words that may have been new to you or used in new ways in *The Watsons Go to Birmingham—1963.*

boycott to refuse to buy something or to take part in something as a way of making a protest

bravo well done!

cockeyed or **lazy-eyed** cross-eyed or having an eye that squints or slants

cracker an offensive term used to describe a class of poor white people in parts of the southeastern United States

discrimination prejudice or unjust behavior to others based on differences in age, race, or gender

egghead a smart person

emulate to follow or imitate

generate to produce or create something

grapevine If you hear information through the grapevine, you hear it unofficially or as a rumor.

hillbilly a negative term used for a person from a backwoods area, especially from the mountains or from the southern United States

imitate to copy or mimic someone or something

jabber to talk in a fast, confused, or foolish way that is hard to understand

jacked up beat up

pan to criticize someone or something harshly

peon a person who does hard or boring work for little or nothing in return

pervasive extending throughout

punctual on time

quest a long search in order to find something

segregate to separate or keep people or things apart

seniority the state of being older or higher in standing

sonic boom the loud noise produced by a vehicle, usually an aircraft, when it travels faster than the speed of sound and breaks the sound barrier

thug a rough, violent person

trespass to enter someone's private property without permission

"Writing to me has always been something that relaxed me. When I was working in the factory, I used to write during breaks because it took me away from being in the factory. I didn't like being there so I would sit down and write. It was much like reading, it would take me away from where I was."

—Christopher Paul Curtis

Christopher Paul Curtis was always a writer. But he never had time to write regularly until he was working on the assembly line at Fisher Body Flint Plant No. 1. He didn't like his job there and found that writing was an escape from the tedious, difficult work. Before he started writing *The Watsons Go to Birmingham—1963,* Curtis hadn't written fiction. "I'd tried fiction, but I knew [my work] was terrible. . . . I didn't really feel comfortable with fiction until my late thirties, early forties."

Though Curtis's books are categorized as children's literature, he has said that when he writes, he doesn't really think about writing specifically for kids. "I know you're supposed to think of your audience, but when I wrote *The Watsons Go to Birmingham—1963*, I didn't really write it as a children's book. I thought of it as a story, and the narrator happened to be ten years old." Of course, the book went on to win many awards in the children's-book industry.

The Watsons are a combination of lots of families that Curtis has known, including his own. "One of the great things about writing," Curtis says, "is that you can use your imagination and you can make all kinds of different combinations of people in situations, and that's what I did with the Watsons."

Creating a character is a key challenge when Curtis is deciding what a book will be about and what will happen in it. Also, research sometimes plays an important part in his writing. With research, he can assure that the historical details are correct. "Once I get the character, everything seems to be okay. It's a mental trick: You actually feel like there's someone talking to you. I just write down what they say. It's very inefficient. I write reams of stuff that I can never use. With *The Watsons*, I didn't have to do a lot of research because I was around [Kenny's age] in 1963."

When he's writing, Curtis has a set pattern to his days. "I'll work at the library usually from about nine to noon, then the next morning, I wake up at five o'clock and I start to edit what I did the day before, try to hammer it down into a story. Writing *The Watsons*, I found that it's better if I just write what comes whether it's going to work at that point in the story or not, then work on cleaning it up the next day. A lot of things come up that I use later on."

Curtis has said that his inspiration for writing is "the love of words and the power they seem to have to be able to change things." He believes that using your own experiences as a resource for your writing is important: "I think it makes your writing more immediate and more believable. There's a truth in it. When you have autobiographical touches in the story it's just more interesting to read."

For aspiring writers

Curtis stresses that young writers, in order to succeed, should write as often as possible. He says,

> The best advice I can give to any aspiring author is to write. Write anytime you have the opportunity. Set up particular times every day when you write and stick to the schedule. I think writing is like any other skill: You have to work at it and you have to practice. It's like an instrument or a sport. The more you do it, the better you're going to get at it. . . . Just the practice of doing it every day makes you better and that's all you can ask for—to slowly develop. It's something that takes a lot of time, so be patient and don't worry if you're not writing stuff that's very good right from the word go. Just keep working at it and things will come around.

But as most writers will tell you, writing is not easy. It demands persistence. "When kids say they don't like what they've written . . . I tell them, 'Be patient. Fiction takes a long time.'" Curtis advises, "Writing is not magical; it's not mystical. Keep it fun. You're in control."

You Be the Author!

• **Keep a daily journal:** Christopher Paul Curtis remarks, "Many times young people feel that writing is, or should be, the result of consultation with some mysterious, hard-to-find muse. I don't think so; I think in many ways writing is much like learning a second language or playing a sport or mastering a musical instrument: The more you do it, the better you become at it. That's why I think keeping a daily journal should be high on the list of priorities for every young writer."

For every writer, it is a good idea to have a convenient place to record observations of the world around you, as well as ideas for stories, characters, and setting.

Using a brand-new notebook or one you already have, start taking a few minutes each day to write down what is going on in the world around you or whatever else crosses your mind. Writing a little bit every day is a great habit to get into!

• **A new end:** Christopher Paul Curtis originally planned for the Watson family to travel to Florida instead of Birmingham, but changed his mind when his son brought home a poem about Birmingham. Is there a place that you know of that you would have liked the Weird Watsons to visit? Write a new ending to the book that includes that place instead of Birmingham.

• **Poems can inspire!:** Christopher Paul Curtis decided to send the Watsons to Birmingham after his son read him "Ballad of Birmingham." Go to the library, check out a book of poems, and find one that is particularly meaningful to you. Perhaps there is a person or place that you feel a connection with in the poem, or maybe you came away from the poem with a new understanding about something. Then, write a story about that person or place or whatever might have drawn you to the poem.

• **Your friends and family are characters:** Is there someone you know who might make a good character in a story or book? Think about what makes that person unique, and how he or she might react to a certain situation. Maybe your mother is a gardener. What if she came across something unusual—fairies, perhaps—in her garden? Write a short story about it.

• **Read all about it:** Design and write your own newspaper. Give it a catchy title, and on the front page, draw a picture of something that happens in *The Watsons Go to Birmingham— 1963*. Write an article to accompany the picture. If you need help, go to the library and look at some of the different ways newspapers attract their readers' attention. For example, your article could be about something serious, like the bombing of the Sixteenth Street Baptist Church, or something funny, like Byron's getting his lips stuck to the mirror of the Brown Bomber.

• **Go back in time:** If you found a time capsule from 1963, what might be in it?

What was important in the news in 1963? To find out, go to the library and look at photographs and articles in newspapers from 1963. Pay special attention to the civil rights movement and the South. You'll see that Christopher Paul Curtis provides historical background about the place and time in his epilogue. But try to take your knowledge a little further. For example, find articles about the church bombings that happened in Birmingham, Alabama.

If you know someone who lived in the South in the 1960s, interview him or her about what life was like in 1963. For fun, you could also find out which movies, books, and television shows were popular that year.

• **Where in the world are the Watsons?:** The Weird Watsons drive from Flint, Michigan, to Birmingham, Alabama, on Interstate 75. As you read the book, look at a road map to track the Watsons' progress. Try to find interesting sites along I-75, perhaps one in each state they would pass through. At the end of the book, answer the following questions:

How many miles did the Watsons travel round trip?

If the Brown Bomber goes only forty-five miles per hour, how long will the trip take?

Did the Watsons take the most direct route to Birmingham? If not, what other highways might they have taken?

• **What are you saying?:** Curtis uses many colloquial (informal and conversational) expressions and words in his writing. As you read, write down some of the different expressions. Try to figure out what the character means from the context in which the expression was used and from other characters' reactions. If you can find a dictionary of regional sayings, that might be helpful to you.

For example, Kenny says, "Dad was going to try to make us forget about being cold by cutting up. Me and Joey started smiling right away, and Byron tried to look cool and bored." Dad, of course, is not actually cutting anything up. We can tell that when he says "cutting up" Kenny means Dad is saying something funny, because he says that he and his sister, Joey, start smiling, and because even this early in the novel we know that Dad is a humorous character.

• **Take the director's seat:** Pretend that *The Watsons Go to Birmingham—1963* is going to be made into a movie. If you were responsible for choosing who would be cast in the movie, whom would you pick to be each of the main characters? Feel free to use famous people or friends or family members. Explain why you made these choices.

• **Chase your blues away:** The Watsons play music on their new record player—the True-Tone AB-700, Ultra-Glide—all the way to Birmingham. Momma likes "Under the Boardwalk," but Kenny prefers "Yakety Yak." Are there any special songs that you listen to when you're feeling down or when you're in a great mood? Make a music mix tape or CD of these songs and copy it for your friends. Ask them to do the same and find out what songs are important to them.

• **Heroes:** In his epilogue, Christopher Paul Curtis writes about heroes, "the boys and girls, the women and men who have seen that things are wrong and have not been afraid to ask 'Why can't we change this?'" Do you know any heroes? Ask your friends and classmates who their heroes are.

Related Reading

Other books by Christopher Paul Curtis

Bud, Not Buddy (1999)

Fiction—African-American

Belle Teal by Ann M. Martin

The Cay by Theodore Taylor

Francie by Karen English

Iggie's House by Judy Blume

The Land; Roll of Thunder, Hear My Cry; Let the Circle Be Unbroken; and *The Road to Memphis* by Mildred D. Taylor

Maniac Magee by Jerry Spinelli

M.C. Higgins, The Great by Virginia Hamilton

Witness by Karen Hesse

Fiction—prejudice

Adaline Falling Star by Mary Pope Osborne

Bat 6 by Virginia Euwer Wolff

Crusader by Edward Bloor

The Divine Wind: A Love Story by Garry Disher

Samir and Yonatan by Daniella Carmi

Saving Shiloh by Phyllis Reynolds Naylor

Nonfiction

The Day Martin Luther King, Jr. Was Shot: A Photo History of the Civil Rights Movement by James Haskins

Free at Last: A History of the Civil Rights Movement and Those Who Died in the Struggle by Sara Bullard

Oh, Freedom! Kids Talk About the Civil Rights Movement with the People Who Made It Happen by Casey King and Linda Barret Osborne

Martin's Big Words by Doreen Rappaport, illustrated by Bryan Collier

Mississippi Challenge by Mildred Pitts Walter

The 1960s by Gini Holland

Separate but Not Equal: The Dream and the Struggle by James Haskins

Movies

Four Little Girls (1997), directed by Spike Lee (available on VHS and DVD)

Books

Curtis, Christopher, Paul. *The Watsons Go to Birmingham—1963.*
    New York: Delacorte Press, 1995.

Newspapers and magazines

The Horn Book Magazine, July/August 2000 issue, pp. 386–396.
The ALAN Review, Winter 1999, Volume 26, Number 2.

Web sites

The ALAN Review:
    http://scholar.lib.vt.edu/ejournals/ALAN/winter99/curtis.html
Children's Book Council/Author-Editor Dialogs: Christopher
    Paul Curtis and Wendy Lamb:
    www.cbcbooks.org/html/curtislamb.html
Educational Paperback Association:
    www.edupaperback.org/showauth.cfm?authid=52
KidsReads.com:
    www.kidsreads.com/authors/au-curtis-christopher-paul.asp
Powell's Books Interviews:
    www.powells.com/authors/curtis.html
Random House:
    www.randomhouse.com/teachers/authors/curtis.html